YOU CAN DRAW
FLOWERS

by Mattia Cerato

PICTURE WINDOW BOOKS
a capstone imprint

MATERIALS

Before you start your amazing drawings, there are a few things you'll need.

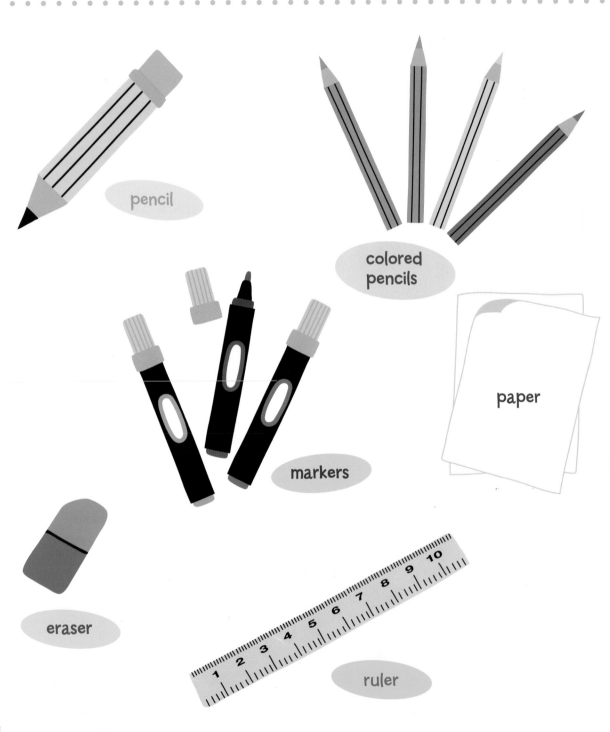

pencil

colored pencils

markers

paper

eraser

ruler

SHAPES

Drawing can be easy! If you can draw these simple letters, numbers, shapes, and lines, YOU CAN DRAW anything in this book.

letters

numbers

DSLU
VZ

123

shapes

lines

Lilac

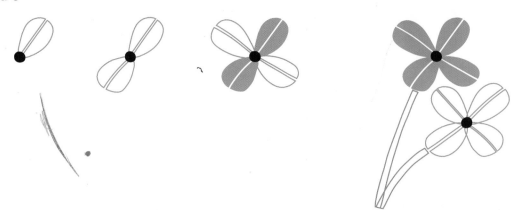

Marigold

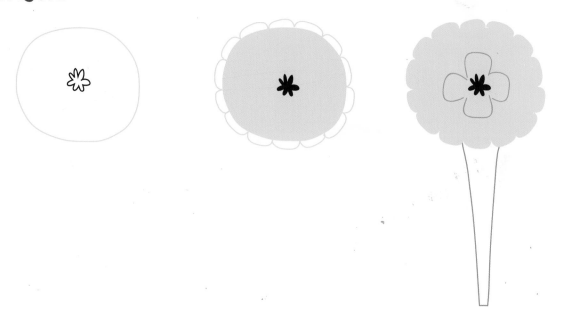

Petunia

5

Water Lily

Forget-Me-Not

    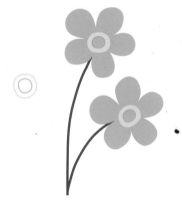

Venus Flytrap

 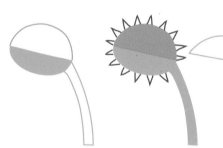 

Violet

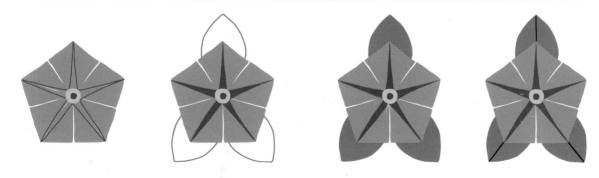

Rose

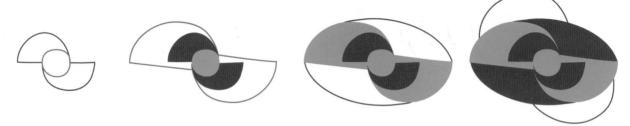

Daisy

 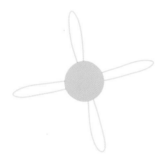 

Pansy

Gladiola

Sunflower

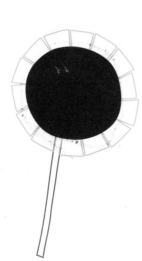

11

Tulips

Jasmine

Rhododendron

Narcissus

Orchid

Daffodils

Dandelion

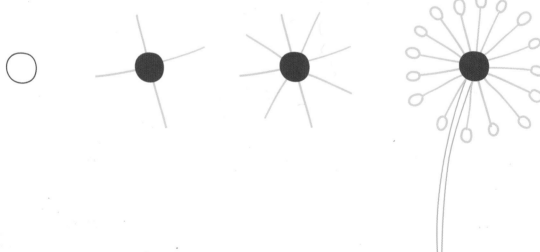

Now try this!

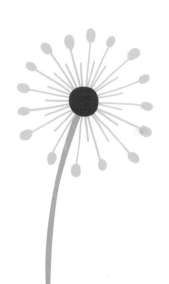

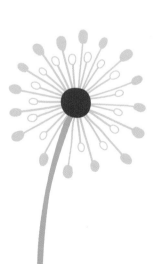

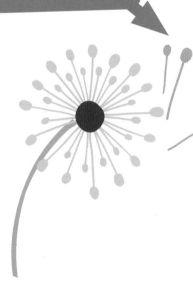

Gardenia

Dahlia

Chrysanthemum

Freesia

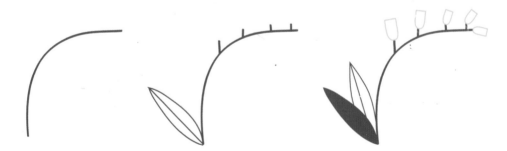

16

Bird of Paradise

Irises

19

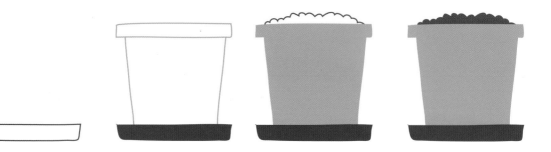

FLOWER POT

BEE

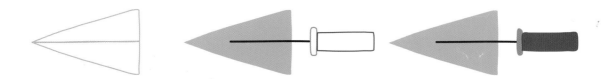

WORM

GARDEN SPADE

20

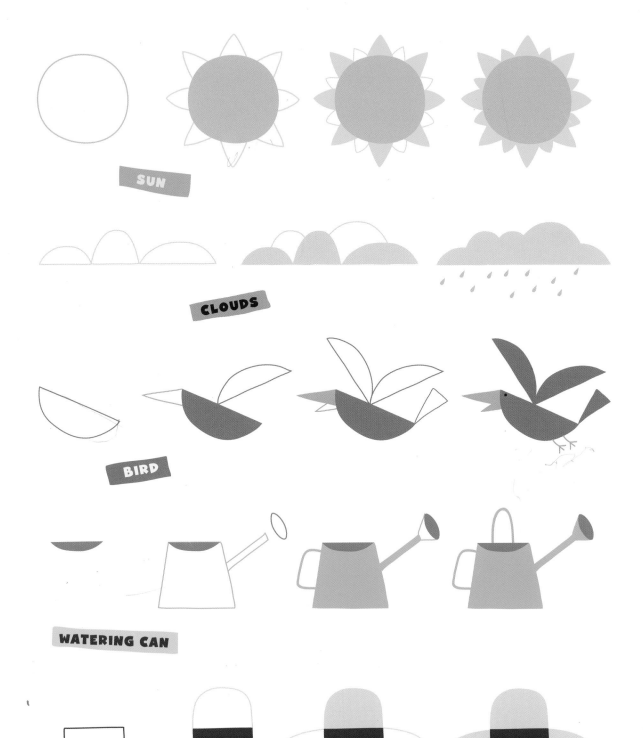

SUN

CLOUDS

BIRD

WATERING CAN

SUN HAT

21

All books published by Picture Window Books
are manufactured with paper containing at least
10 percent post-consumer waste.

Library of Congress Cataloging-in-Publication Data
Cerato, Mattia.
  You can draw flowers / by Mattia Cerato ; illustrated by Mattia Cerato.
     p. cm. — (You can draw)
  Includes index.
  ISBN 978-1-4048-6279-1 (library binding)
  1. Flowers in art—Juvenile literature. 2.
Drawing—Technique—Juvenile literature. I. Cerato, Mattia. II. Title.
  NC815.B78 2011
  743'.73—dc22
                            2010030033

Printed in the United States of America in North Mankato, Minnesota.
092010
005933CGS11

Picture Window Books
151 Good Counsel Drive
P.O. Box 669
Mankato, MN 56002-0669
877-845-8392
www.capstonepub.com

Editor: Shelly Lyons
Designer: Matt Bruning
Art Director: Nathan Gassman
Production Specialist: Sarah Bennett
The illustrations in this book were created digitally.

Internet Sites •

FactHound offers a safe, fun way to find Internet sites related to this book.
All of the sites on FactHound have been researched by our staff.

Here's all you do:

Visit *www.facthound.com*

Type in this code: 9781404862791

 Check out projects, games and lots more at
www.capstonekids.com

Look for all the books in the You Gan Draw series: